Hurricanes

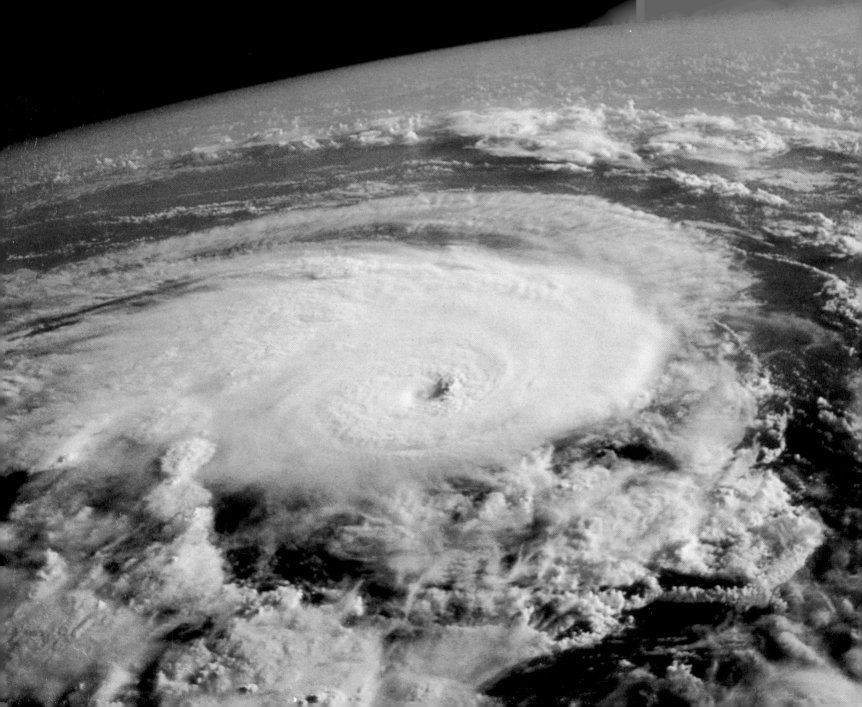

Hurricanes

by D. M. Souza

NATURE IN ACTION

Carolrhoda Books, Inc./Minneapolis

The publisher wishes to thank Professor Jonathan Kahl, Department of Geosciences, University of Wisconsin–Milwaukee, for his assistance in the preparation of this manuscript.

This book is available in two editions:
Library binding by Carolrhoda Books, Inc.
Soft cover by First Avenue Editions
Carolrhoda Books, Inc., and First Avenue Editions
c / o The Lerner Group
241 First Avenue North, Minneapolis, MN 55401

LIBRARY OF CONGRESS CATALOGING-IN-PUBLICATION DATA

Souza, D. M. (Dorothy M.)
    Hurricanes / by D. M. Souza.
      p.   cm. — (Nature in action)
    Includes index.
    ISBN 0-87614-861-5 (lib. bdg.)
    ISBN 0-87614-955-7 (pbk.)
    1. Hurricanes—Juvenile literature. [1. Hurricanes.] I. Title.
    II. Series: Nature in action (Minneapolis, Minn.)
    QC944.2.S68 1996
    551.55′2—dc20   94-21143
                                                          CIP
                                                          AC

Manufactured in the United States of America
1 2 3 4 5 6 – JR – 01 00 99 98 97 96

Contents

Hurricanes can cause enormous damage when they move onto land. Here, residents of a building in Miami, Florida, return to what's left of their home after Hurricane Andrew struck.

Gentle breezes scatter leaves and seeds, lift kites high in the sky, and bring cool air in from the ocean. But not all breezes are gentle. Powerful winds uproot tall trees, whip up giant waves, and drive storms miles across the Earth.

Many strong winds begin at sea. They whirl over the waters like enormous spinning tops, howling and screaming as they spin. If these winds move onto land, they may bring floods, level cities and villages, and claim many lives.

5

A typhoon in progress

In different parts of the world, these storms have different names. In the Indian Ocean and around Australia, they're called cyclones. In the Pacific, they're known as typhoons. If they appear in the Atlantic Ocean, the Caribbean or the Gulf of Mexico, we call them hurricanes. Scientists call all of these storms tropical cyclones.

The word *hurricane* comes from Huracán, the god of stormy weather, whom native peoples of the Caribbean islands once feared.

6

A thunderstorm over the Caribbean Sea. Hurricanes begin as storms over the ocean.

What is a Hurricane?

A hurricane is a huge storm with winds that blow faster than 74 miles per hour. It is packed with very heavy rains and towering thunderclouds.

For days this monster spins across warm tropical seas. If the waters along the hurricane's path become warmer, the storm may grow larger and stronger. Not until it passes over cooler waters or crosses land will it break apart and die.

What makes the hurricane winds blow? Why do they spin the way they do, and how do the thunderclouds form? Let's find out by first discovering a few things about wind and thunderclouds.

Wind

Everything in the universe, whether it is a solid, a liquid, or a gas, is made up of tiny particles known as atoms. The air around you, for example, contains atoms of many different gases. These atoms are all joined together in clusters known as molecules.

When air is warmed, its molecules bounce around faster and faster and move farther apart. The air then becomes light, and it rises. If air is cooled, the molecules press closer together. Then the air becomes heavy, and it sinks.

As air moves, it pushes against things. At this very moment, millions of molecules of air are pushing against your body like tiny, invisible balls. You don't feel them—they're too small. But if you perform a simple experiment, you'll see just how strong the pressure of air is.

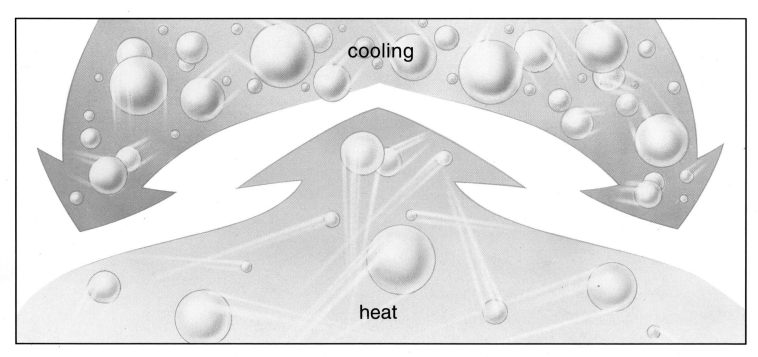

Molecules of air move apart as they are heated, and press close together as they cool.

Fill a plastic cup with water and lay a piece of cardboard or a postcard over the top of the glass. Holding the card in place with one hand, turn the glass upside down over a sink. Next, carefully remove your hand from the cardboard or postcard. The molecules of air pushing against the card should keep the water from spilling out of the glass.

When air is cool, its pressure is usually high. When air is warm, its pressure is usually low.

Air pressure is measured with a device called a barometer.

Every day, different places on Earth receive different amounts of sunshine, and this causes huge masses of warm and cold air to collect in different places around the world. These masses may be thousands of miles wide and may extend 8 to 10 miles up into the atmosphere. The masses of cold and warm air form high and low pressure systems.

Two low pressure systems, as seen by a satellite in space

Sunshine and blue skies usually mean that a high pressure system is present, but thick clouds may signal that a low pressure system is moving in.

The presence of a high pressure system, or high, usually means that the weather will be pleasant. A low may signal the coming of a storm.

Air moves from an area of high pressure toward one of low pressure, like water flowing downhill (from a high place to a low place). We feel this movement and call it the wind.

If the difference in pressure between the high and low is small, a slight breeze blows. If the difference is large, strong gusts howl.

Wind Direction

Around the equator, halfway between the North and South Poles, the Sun's rays are the hottest. In this area, known as the tropics, warm air is constantly rising, and cool air from the poles is always moving in to replace it. But the two masses of air do not travel in straight lines north and south. The rotation, or spinning, of the Earth makes the air masses change directions.

In tropical regions, the sun's rays are at their hottest.

Imagine being in the middle of a large skating rink. If you wanted to get to a bench on the north edge of the rink, you would simply skate straight toward it. But if the rink began spinning, you would have to skate sideways to reach the bench. You would curve to the right or the left, depending on which way the rink was turning.

The same thing happens to large masses of air. As they move from the equator to the poles and back again, the Earth is turning faster than the air is moving. (At the equator, the Earth spins from west to east at about 1,000 miles per hour.) Like the skater, winds curve sideways. Their curving is known as the Coriolis force. Winds moving north and south curve so much they end up coming from the west or east.

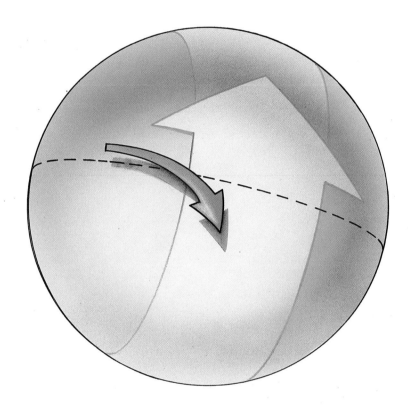

The turning of Earth not only changes the paths taken by north and south winds, it also affects the way masses of high and low pressure move. North of the equator, air in a high turns in a clockwise direction because of the Coriolis force. For the same reason, the air spins counterclockwise in a low. South of the equator, highs and lows move in the opposite directions.

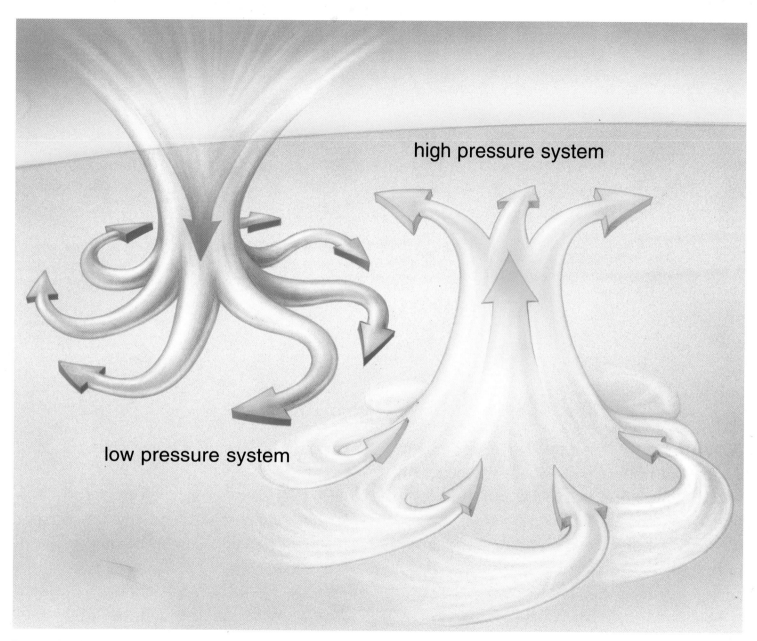

high pressure system

low pressure system

Left: The Coriolis force causes winds to curve as they move north and south from the equator toward the poles. **Right:** Because of the Coriolis force, air spins in different directions around high and low pressure systems.

Thunderclouds

You know the way tiny clouds sometimes appear when you blow your warm breath into cold air. Similar clouds will also float over a kettle of boiling water. What makes these miniature clouds form? The same heating and cooling of air that makes giant clouds appear in the sky.

When water is heated, its molecules begin to move around quickly and stray farther apart. Some break away and fly into the air. They evaporate, or turn into an invisible gas called water vapor.

Vapor is always rising up from the Earth and entering the air. The amount of vapor present in the air at any given time is known as humidity.

We can't see the vapor until air is heated. Then, as warm air rises and cools, the vapor condenses, or changes back into a liquid. Small droplets of water reappear and form a cloud.

Clouds of many different shapes and sizes fill the sky from time to time, but the giants of them all are the thunderclouds, or cumulonimbus clouds. They reach from just above ground level to more than 35,000 feet in the air. They are filled with tremendous amounts of heat energy.

Where does this energy come from? Suppose that on a hot summer day, someone turns a spray of water on you. The drops covering you will soon evaporate, but to do so, they need heat energy. They get it from your warm body. This is why you feel cooler after being sprayed.

A growing thundercloud

When drops of water evaporate above the Earth, they get their heat energy from the warm air around them. If they cool and condense again, they release this energy, which is called latent heat.

Now imagine billions of molecules of water vapor rising in the air and changing back again into drops of water. As this happens, huge amounts of latent heat are thrown off. This heat warms the surrounding air in the cloud and pushes it higher and higher in gusts, or updrafts. The cloud grows taller and taller.

Cool, heavier air blasts downward inside the cloud in a downdraft. Updrafts and downdrafts become stronger and stronger. They can be powerful enough to tear apart a large aircraft.

Now droplets of water begin banging into one another. They become larger and heavier, and begin to fall to the ground as rain. Soon torrents of rain are falling. Lightning flashes and thunder rumbles. The thundercloud fills the sky.

Each day, thousands of these clouds form in different parts of the world. They appear most frequently during the hot months. If they develop over warm ocean water, a violent hurricane may result.

How Does a Hurricane Develop?

Before a hurricane can form, the ocean waters must reach temperatures of between 79° and 80° F. Air near the ocean's surface must be filled with moisture. Also, winds must be coming together from different directions, or converging.

During the warm summer and fall months, the sun beats down almost continually on the ocean waters in the tropics. Warm, moist air rises above the waters and drifts skyward. Cooler air from above moves in to take the place of the rising warm air. This cooler air begins spinning counterclockwise around the newly developing storm. As warm air continues to rise, the pressure drops, making the winds blow stronger.

More moisture evaporates from the sea, rises, and condenses. The heat energy it gives off pushes the air inside the low even higher. Towering thunderclouds form, and rain falls in heavy sheets. Soon clouds, rain, and air are caught up in a huge wheel that, because of the Coriolis force, begins spinning. As long as ocean waters remain warm and winds keep whirling, the storm grows in size and strength.

Warm ocean temperatures and tropical thunderstorms often lead to hurricanes developing.

If the winds are blowing at 38 miles per hour or less, the storm is classified as a tropical depression. If the winds are between 39 and 73 miles per hour, the disturbance is called a tropical storm. When the winds reach speeds of 74 miles per hour or greater, a hurricane is born.

This large cumulonimbus cloud is part of a tropical storm.

What Does a Hurricane Look Like?

You cannot see a hurricane all at once because it is too large. Only if you fly above it or see pictures taken from a satellite in space will you have some idea of its mammoth size. The whirling mass, shaped like a donut, may be 200 to 600 miles wide (300 miles is typical) and reach 40,000 to 50,000 feet up into the sky.

A photograph of Hurricane Bonnie, in 1992, taken from a satellite in space

Power lines and trees can be easily blown down by hurricane winds.

Near a hurricane, winds are light and the sky is covered with a veil of thin, high clouds. Inside the storm, however, the weather becomes more and more violent, until it explodes in the eye wall.

The eye wall is a ring of fierce thunderstorms surrounding the center of the hurricane. As air rushes toward this center, it becomes packed with water vapor. The vapor rises rapidly and condenses, forming towering thunderstorms. Here rainfall is heaviest. Billions of tons of water that have been sucked up from the sea pour out of the clouds.

Within the eye wall, winds are at their strongest. They scream and swirl around so furiously that it is difficult to breathe, see, or hear. Over the ocean, these winds may stir up waves that are taller than three-story buildings. Over land, they uproot trees, tear apart homes, and cause widespread destruction.

Hurricane Hugo, in 1989, was powerful enough to tear apart these buildings in Charleston, South Carolina.

Sunshine can be seen inside the eye of Hurricane Allen.

The eye, or center, of the storm, which is next to the eye wall, is an area of surprising calm. As air in the warm center pushes against the thunderclouds, it creates this nearly cloud-free space. It is filled with light breezes and clear skies.

The size of the eye depends on the strength of the winds surrounding it. The stronger they are, the more tightly they wrap themselves around the eye, and the smaller it becomes. Most eyes are about 20 miles wide. They are usually oval in shape but can also be round.

Even though the eye of a hurricane is calm and sunny, the space can be dangerous. Often, people are fooled into thinking that the hurricane has passed. They come out of their homes or shelters, and suddenly the wall of clouds, the fierce winds, and the downpour return. The other side of the swirling mass arrives, and the storm is as violent as it was before.

When and Where Do Hurricanes Form?

During those times of the year when the seas are at their warmest and the air above them becomes heavy with moisture, the hurricane season begins in the tropics. The only ocean where these storms do not appear is the South Atlantic. Scientists are still not certain why this is.

Over the western Pacific, storms usually form from June through October. Along the Atlantic and Gulf coasts, they generally appear from June through November. Any time the seas are warm and the air is humid, however, hurricanes can develop. In 1955, for example, Tropical Storm Alice grew into a hurricane on January 4.

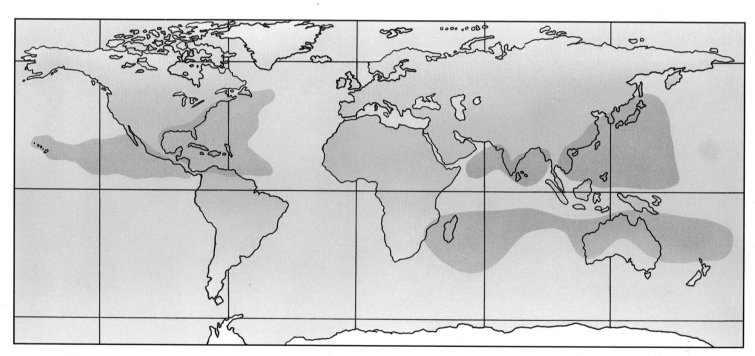

The shaded areas represent the main regions of hurricane activity around the world.

Frequently, June and July storms that affect the United States begin in the Gulf of Mexico and the Caribbean Sea. In August, as parts of the Atlantic Ocean warm up, storms develop farther out at sea. Here, because of the large body of water, they also increase in size and activity. Early September is the height of hurricane season. In October the storms again return to the Caribbean and the Gulf of Mexico.

Many hurricanes that head toward the United States start as far away as the Cape Verde Islands, off the coast of West Africa. Here small thunderstorms develop, clump together, and whirl around as one large storm. Hurricane Andrew started in this region in 1992.

Some hurricanes last for only a few hours, while others twist and turn for several weeks. In 1971, Hurricane Ginger raged for 20 days before falling apart 11 days later. Most storms, however, die out in less than a week.

What Makes a Hurricane Move?

Many hurricanes that begin north of the equator are pushed westward by winds that are blowing only 10 to 15 miles per hour. If the winds blow faster, the storms move too quickly to gather the strength needed to develop into hurricanes.

Sometimes a storm is pushed directly toward the United States. But before it strikes, air currents steer it over cooler waters. There, instead of picking up strength as it would over warm waters, it weakens and falls apart.

A hurricane forming over the ocean, as seen from space

Some of the damage done by
Hurricane Hugo

Sometimes a storm moves westward across the ocean, and air currents turn it northward. As it moves, it brushes states along the Atlantic coastline. In 1989, for example, Hurricane Hugo struck the Carolinas. And in 1991, Hurricane Bob swept off roofs as far north as the state of Maine.

No two hurricanes follow the same path. Some move like straight arrows. Others curve like fishhooks. Still others take loop-the-loop paths. Air currents and high and low pressure systems all play a part in determining which way the storms go.

28

A resident of Dauphin Island, off the coast of Alabama, in what was left of her living room after Hurricane Elena struck the island in September 1985

One of the most unpredictable hurricanes to hit the United States was Hurricane Elena. In 1985 the storm entered the Gulf of Mexico and headed toward the tip of Florida. People there were evacuated. Then slowly Elena turned toward Tampa Bay, and more people had to be evacuated. But Elena changed course once again and finally came ashore over parts of Mississippi and Louisiana. Fortunately, residents there had also been evacuated.

29

What Happens When a Hurricane Strikes Land?

Hurricane Andrew did tremendous damage to homes and other buildings, including this mobile home park in Homestead, Florida, when it moved onto land in September 1992.

Over a period of five years, an average of three hurricanes will strike the United States. The damage done can be widespread.

Powerful winds can rip off roofs, topple trees and power poles, and turn anything that is loose into a weapon of destruction. Lawn chairs, bicycles, even small toys fly through the air with the speed of bullets. Hurricane Andrew, in 1992, ripped an 80-foot steel beam weighing several tons off a building and flung it more than a block away.

Some hurricanes also stir up tornadoes. Nearly a quarter of the storms produce powerful tornadoes, an average of 10 each. In 1967 Hurricane Beulah was responsible for 141 tornadoes tearing across Texas.

Heavy rains often cause severe flooding. A typical hurricane may bring 6 to 12 inches of rain in a single day! During Hurricane Camille, in 1969, over 27 inches of rain fell in 8 hours in parts of Virginia.

Hurricanes cause severe flooding *(below)* and can sometimes produce tornadoes *(right)*.

Storm Surge

The greatest destructive force, however, comes from what is known as a storm surge. It claims 9 out of 10 victims in a typical hurricane.

While the storm is still over the ocean, higher pressure pushes down on the water surrounding the eye. Below the eye, where the pressure is lowest, the ocean rises. Water rises as if it were being sucked into a giant straw. When the eye comes ashore, this mound of water, called the storm surge, unleashes its power. The lower the pressure in the eye, the greater the surge.

As the wall of water crashes onto land, it not only floods coastal towns and cities, but pushes extra water into bays, rivers, and creeks, making them overflow.

Albany, Georgia, was heavily flooded as a result of Tropical Storm Alberto in July 1994.

The worst storm surge to hit the United States came with Hurricane Camille in 1969. It pushed parts of the Gulf of Mexico 3 feet higher than normal. Water at Pass Christian, Mississippi, rose more than 20 feet above its normal level. Thousands of homes and businesses were destroyed. Many of the 256 people who lost their lives in the storm were victims of the surge.

Predicting the likely course of a hurricane and warning residents of its approach is the difficult task of scientists at the National Hurricane Center in Coral Gables, Florida.

Forecasting Hurricanes

When a tropical disturbance appears in the Atlantic Ocean, the Caribbean Sea, or the Gulf of Mexico, scientists at the National Hurricane Center are placed on alert. With the aid of weather satellites, which observe Earth's weather from space, they pinpoint the location of the disturbance. Weather balloons, equipped with measuring instruments, are launched twice a day around the world and help scientists spot changes in temperature and water vapor in the atmosphere.

The National Hurricane Center, in Coral Gables, Florida

35

A scientist follows the progress of Hurricane Allen in June 1987.

If the disturbance grows into a tropical storm, the scientists give it a name. This name is taken from a list of 21 common male and female names. A different list is used each year for 6 years, then the lists are repeated. Once a storm causes severe damage, its name is removed from the list and no longer used.

Some names that are no longer on the list are Andrew (1992); Bob (1991); Hugo (1989); Joan (1988); and Gilbert (1988).

Once a storm has been named, pilots known as hurricane hunters are given the dangerous job of tracking it.

Hurricane Hunters

Two giant four-engine planes are stationed at the United States Air Force base near Biloxi, Mississippi. Another similar aircraft is based at Miami International Airport. Crew members of these planes are trained to gather information on hurricanes, with the help of special equipment on board. When they receive orders, they head for the eye of the storm.

The pilot of a hurricane hunter plane prepares to fly into a hurricane.

Powerful winds batter the plane continually. Everyone must be strapped into a safety harness, and all equipment must be tied down.

As the plane approaches the eye wall, rain comes in torrents, and strong updrafts and downdrafts toss the aircraft around as if it were a toy. Lightning may rip through the sky.

After what must seem like hours, the plane enters the eye and begins circling the calm, clear center. Members of the crew plot the location of the eye and the speed of the wind. They throw out a small parachute with a metal cylinder called a dropsonde attached. The dropsonde contains instruments that measure pressure, temperature, and humidity as the cylinder falls toward the sea. This information is later used by the scientists at the National Hurricane Center. They feed it into computers, along with images received from satellites and reports from ships. From all of this data, when they attempt to forecast where the hurricane is headed, when it will arrive, and how strong it will be. The task is challenging because at any moment the storm may change course due to changing air currents or pressure systems. Then a new forecast must be issued.

Opposite page: A close-up view of the eye and eye wall of Hurricane Allen, from a hurricane hunter plane. **Above:** A gust probe, a device once used for research, and now used as a lightning rod for hurricane hunter planes

Watches and Warnings

If a hurricane appears to be moving toward land, forecasters send out a notice called a hurricane watch. This alerts people in an area that they may be threatened. If the storm looks as if it will strike within 24 hours or less, a hurricane warning is given.

Forecasters are very careful about issuing watches and warnings. Preparing for a hurricane is difficult and expensive. To evacuate people from an area, board up homes and offices, close down businesses, and take other steps to prevent hurricane damage can cost millions of dollars. If the storm does not arrive as predicted, people may be less likely to pay attention the next time a warning is given. Scientists try to be as certain as they can be about where and when a hurricane will strike before they issue watches and warnings.

Shop owners in New Orleans board up their windows to prepare for Hurricane Andrew in August 1992.

Improvements in forecasting have helped save many lives. In 1900, the deadliest hurricane on record in the United States killed 6,000 people in Galveston, Texas. In 1992, because of advance warnings, thousands of people were evacuated before Hurricane Andrew hit, and only 26 lives were lost.

The risk of property damage, however, is higher than ever due to the large numbers of people now living in areas along the Gulf of Mexico and the Atlantic coast. In 1989, for example, destruction from Hurricane Hugo totaled about $7 billion. In 1992, losses from Hurricane Andrew were between $20 and $25 billion. Forecasters can do nothing to prevent this costly destruction.

Left: The Galveston, Texas, hurricane of 1900 was the deadliest ever in the United States. **Below**: Hurricane Hugo damaged property throughout the West Indies and the southeastern United States. Coastal areas, particularly in South Carolina, suffered the worst damage.

Hurricane Safety

Once a watch has been issued in your area, remember that you still have more than 24 hours before you will know if the storm is headed your way. Stay calm and listen to the radio or television for updated bulletins.

If you live on an island, near a coastline or river, or in a mobile home, you and hundreds of others may have to be evacuated. Get an early start. In a short time, roads and highways could be jammed with traffic.

If a warning is given, listen carefully to directions and follow them immediately. If you do not have to leave, several steps will have to be taken. Try to be as helpful as you can.

As you can see from the damage that Hurricane Andrew did to this mobile home park in Homestead, Florida, mobile homes are dangerous places to be during hurricanes.

In September 1992, these people in Savannah, Georgia, were filling their propane tanks in case Hurricane Hugo knocked out their electricity later that day.

Lawn furniture, bicycles, toys, or anything else outside that might blow away, should be put in a safe place. During storms, water mains sometimes break, so containers should be filled with enough drinking water to last for several days. Pets should be put in safe places with plenty of food and water close by.

Once the storm arrives, stay indoors and away from walls and windows that might collapse or be blown away. If it is night, have a flashlight close by. In case of a power failure, you will then have a light to help you see your way around.

Don't use the phone unless it is necessary. Many people may be trying to make emergency calls, and phone lines may even be knocked down in some areas.

Once the "All Clear" is given on the radio or television or by local officials, be careful if you have to go outside. Stay away from downed power poles, dangerous live wires, dangling tree branches, and broken water or sewer mains. Tell an adult about any damages you see.

Hurricanes are powerful and frightening events. A single hurricane stirs up millions of miles of air and dumps huge amounts of rain wherever it goes. Waters far beneath the surface of the sea are churned up, and the waves that are created may last long after the giant wheel of wind and thunderclouds has passed.

Fascinating Facts

In 1502 adventurers in search of gold set out for the Americas during hurricane season. Twenty ships were caught in a storm, and 19 of them sank off the coast of Puerto Rico.

During hurricanes, waves frequently toss tons of gasping fish onto beaches. The eyes of many of them have popped out because of sudden changes in pressure.

Birds from the West Indies have sometimes been blown into southern Florida by the force of the winds. Others have landed exhausted on the decks of ships that survived the storms.

A palm forest in Puerto Rico, damaged by Hurricane Hugo. Islands in the Caribbean are often hit by hurricanes.

Damage from Hurricane Camille, in 1969

On the shores of Honduras, a large grove of coconut trees is said to have grown after a hurricane washed ashore seeds from coconuts that were on board a sunken ship.

According to some Pacific islanders, a normally white plant that grows in their area turns red during hurricane season.

Hurricane winds can make the walls of houses move in and out as if they were breathing. The force of a storm can turn water along coastlines purple with churned mud and sea plants during hurricanes.

Since pilots first began flying into typhoons and hurricanes in 1943, only three planes have been lost in the storms. No trace of these planes or their crews has ever been found.

Glossary

Barometer: an instrument used to measure air pressure

Condensation: the process by which water vapor cools and becomes liquid water

Converging: coming together from different directions

Coriolis force: a force created by the Earth's rotation that causes winds to curve

Dropsonde: a device containing instruments used to gather information about weather conditions

Evaporation: the process by which liquids turn into gases when heated

Eye wall: a ring of strong thunderstorms surrounding the eye of a hurricane

Eye: an area of calm winds within the center of a hurricane

Humidity: the amount of water vapor present in the air

Latent heat: heat energy given off by water as it cools and condenses

Storm surge: a wall of ocean water that rises as a result of a hurricane and overflows onto land. The storm surge is often the most destructive part of a hurricane.

Tropical cyclone: the term that scientists use to describe hurricane-type storms

Tropical depression: a storm formed at sea and producing winds of 38 miles per hour or less

Tropical storm: a storm formed at sea and producing winds of 39 to 73 miles per hour

Water vapor: water in the form of a gas, produced when water is heated to a high temperature

Index

air pressure, 8–9, 10, 18, 24, 33
Atlantic Ocean, 25, 26, 35, 41

Caribbean Sea, 6, 7, 26, 35, 45
clouds, 14–15, 18, 22, 24; formation of, 14; thunderclouds, 7, 15, 16, 17, 24
Coriolis force, 12–13, 18
cumulonimbus clouds, 15, 20. *See also* thunderclouds.

equator, 11, 12, 27
eye wall, 22
eye, 24, 33, 37

floods, 5, 32, 33, 34
formation of hurricanes, 18, 20, 25–26, 27

Gulf of Mexico, 6, 25, 26, 29, 35, 41

high pressure systems, 9–10, 28
Hurricane Allen, 24, 36
Hurricane Andrew, 5, 27, 30, 36, 40, 41
Hurricane Bob, 28, 36
Hurricane Camille, 32, 34
hurricane damage, 5, 22, 23, 28, 29, 30, 32, 33, 34, 36, 40, 41, 42
Hurricane Elena, 29
Hurricane Ginger, 26
Hurricane Hugo, 23, 28, 36, 41, 45
hurricane hunters, 36–39
hurricane safety, 40, 41, 42–44

Indian Ocean, 6

latent heat, 16, 18
lightning, 17, 39
low pressure systems, 9–10, 28

movement of air, 10, 11, 14, 18, 28
movement of hurricanes, 5, 27–29

naming of hurricanes, 36
National Hurricane Center, 34, 35–36, 39

ocean temperature, 7, 17, 18, 25

Pacific Ocean, 6, 25

rain, 17, 18, 22, 24, 32

storm surge, 33, 34

thunderstorms, 7, 17, 18, 22
tornadoes, 32
tropical depression, 20
tropical storm, 20, 36

water vapor, 14, 16, 22, 35
weather forecasts, 39, 40, 41, 44
winds, 5, 7, 8, 10, 11, 22, 24, 30; convergence of, 18; speed of, 20, 27

METRIC CONVERSION CHART To find measurements that are almost equal		
WHEN YOU KNOW:	**MULTIPLY BY:**	**TO FIND:**
inches	2.54	centimeters
feet	30.48	centimeters
yards	0.91	meters
miles	1.61	kilometers